Апиреа Deлога

Revelation

Promises Along the Way

Exhilarating Journey:
Book 2

By: Anysia Derora

All scripture verses are from the Amplified Bible, unless otherwise noted.

"Everlasting Journey" Dedication

I dedicate the "Exhilarating Journey" series to Jesus, without Whom I would not be here to write it. He is my Friend, my Love, my King, my Champion, the One Who cared enough to invite me on this journey in the first place and the One Who continues to invite me further and deeper. He is my Guide in the amazing off-the-map places of life and the One with Whom I share the wonder and splendor of the discovery process. He never ceases to amaze me. I am blessed to be His and to be journeying with Him on this truly Exhilarating Journey.

"Revelation" Dedication

I dedicate "Revelation" to all of those who have set their hearts, minds and affection on knowing the Lord and becoming all they behold in His eyes.

Introduction

Have you ever asked yourself the question: "What if there's more to this life than what I'm living?"

Have you felt the stirring to explore territory you've never seen and aren't sure is even there? Is there something in your heart that just knows that you are meant for something greater and more significant than what you're doing and experiencing right now? Do you long for adventure but wonder where to find it? Is there a stirring in your heart to see your story be one of impact, discovery, and wonder?

If so, then I have great news for you! There is a place in the Kingdom with your name on it. A place that is more expansive and amazing than you can even imagine. A place that God Himself has set aside for you as your inheritance and He is inviting you on the journey to discover and explore this rich, land of promise that is yours.

There is a precipice where God wants you to stand, overlooking all the promise and provision that is yours in the Kingdom; a view of life and freedom that He wants to give you that will turn your perspective upside down and give you a new lens through which to view everything in your life. He invites you to stand in that place, stake your claim and explore the height, length, width and breadth of the glory that He desires to usher you into.

The poems, songs, scriptures, stories and prophecies in this four-book series are invitations to you to step over the threshold of the life the world tries to hold you in and into the unlimited possibilities of the place of God's presence; the place you were created to live, move and have your being. There is majesty, wonder, splendor and radiance beyond your wildest dreams just waiting for you to take that step. I invite you to take God's hand and partner with Him on the adventure of lifetime!

Hebrews 11:8

[Urged on] by faith Abraham, when he was called, obeyed and went forth to a place which he was destined to receive as an inheritance and he went, although he did not know or trouble his mind about where he was to go.

About this Book

The book you hold in your hands is unique. It is a combination of story; nuggets to stir your heart; prophetic words from the Lord, personal testimonies, poetry and songs – each piece selected specifically to encourage you on your journey into a deeper relationship with the Lord.

Except for poetry and songs, which are self-evident, the other portions of this book are marked with specific pictures to indicate what you are reading:

Story: Each of the four books in this series begins with a chapter of the Exhilarating Journey story associated with that section. The four books are: Invitation, Revelation, Adoration, Culmination.

Nuggets: The Nuggets are spread throughout the book. Their purpose is to stir your heart; to ask questions that challenge you to think in new and different ways. Many of these are excerpts from my own journals – responses to things God has said or done on my own journey which I felt might also encourage others. Take them for a spin in your gold mining pan and see where they take you.

Keys: The Keys are prophetic words from the Lord. These are words He has spoken to me over the years; invitations; encouragement; revelation and simple notes of love and reminders of the value He sees in each of us. May they encourage your heart and draw you nearer to His.

Testimonies: The Testimonies are stories from my own journey with the Lord over the years. These personal stories are some of the landmarks along the way; times I look back on to encourage myself in God's faithfulness. And, while He certainly deals with each of us uniquely, He also doesn't play favorites.

How you approach this book is entirely up to you. You can read it morsel by morsel in order or jump around. You may want to devour it beginning to end and then re-approach it slowly and deliberately, revisiting those places that touched your heart or challenged your thinking.

No matter how you approach it, my hope is that you will return to the page's time and again on your own journey into knowing God, and in the process, discover who He created you to be.

I hope that if I ever meet you and you have any of the books in this series in your possession that I will find notes that you've written as a result of your own exploration. That you will share with me the fresh revelation the Lord gave to you as you said "yes" to the journey with Him.

I do not present this to you as a complete journey, instead I present it to you as a prayer and an urging to hear the voice of the Lord calling you off the map and into an exhilarating journey that will change the course of your life and the lives of those around you forever.

Anysia Derora

07.07.2016

Story: Revelation – Promises Along the Way

*N*othing visible changed as she placed her hand in His, yet everything was different. As she looked into His eyes and saw her own reflection there, her heart was ignited.

How was this possible? How was it that One so perfect and amazing and wonderful could love her so deeply and see her so very differently than she saw herself? Was it a dream? A fools hope for a life that could never be? Or was it an invitation beyond her wildest imagining to become what she was beholding in His eyes? Could it really be?

His smile intoxicated her. How had she not noticed how engaging He was? How strong and gentle? How utterly attentive to her? Her thoughts of doubt, fear and worthlessness drowned in the endless magnificence of the unfathomable love that radiated from His smile, His eyes, His touch.

And then…He spoke… *"I love you, My cherished one. I have so longed to take this journey with you. To show you Who I am and to disclose to you who we are together. I long to show you who you were created to be and to hold your hand as you become all you behold along the way. There is a fire in you I wish to awaken; a passion awaiting My breath; a purpose awaiting My vision. Come, see what I see. Come, hear what I hear. Come, let Me show you what abundant life really looks like."*

As He spoke, His words washed over her in refreshing waves, filling her with confidence and expectation. She took a step closer to that beautiful face and reached out her hand to touch His cheek. He kissed the palm of her hand and embraced her. *"This is a journey to My heart, Beloved; and a journey to yours. A journey of discovery and revelation that will leave you breathless with awe and wonder."*

Finding her voice, at last, she asked, "Will it always be like this?"

His smile warmed her, *"No. There will be days you won't see Me or feel My presence but know this for certain I will be with you always. Do not fear. Hold fast to the Truth that I love you. I will give you promises along the way and know this…while others have lied to you and made promises they did not or could not keep – I am not a man that I should lie, nor the son of man that I should change My mind. Every promise I give to you is yours. I watch over My word to perform it and I will bring it to pass as I have said. I do not disappoint. Watch for My promises. Listen to My heart for you as we venture together off the map of the ordinary and predictable; and into the extraordinary life of amazement, glory and discovery. A life where the Holy Spirit takes all that is Mine and discloses it to you, so that you may experience the lavish extravagance of My passion for you. In every situation, in every circumstance, know that there is an encounter with My heart awaiting – a promise of greater intimacy and revelation than you have ever known before."*

Alight with the certainty of His promise, she melted into His embrace and set her heart to the compass of the Love she knew, at last, could not fail.

There is a fire in you I wish to awaken;

a passion awaiting My breath;

a purpose awaiting My vision.

2nd Corinthians 1:20

For as many as are the promises of God, they all find their Yes [answer] in Him [Christ]. For this reason, we also utter the Amen (so be it) to God through Him [in His Person and by His agency] to the glory of God.

Testimony: Command the Rain

*I*n 2005 the Lord had told me to return to Tampa to finish Bible School. The whole move was a testimony of His goodness and faithfulness. One day I was in Juneau, Alaska attending revival meetings, a week later I was flying from Portland, OR to Tampa, FL with just what I could carry – no place to live, no car, a bag of change, enough money for one night's hotel stay and a $100 post-dated check. I was staying in a hotel almost 2 miles from the church and school but figured I could easily walk that and was just believing that God would provide somewhere for me to stay quickly.

Sunday morning, when I woke up, I knew it was going to rain while I was walking to church. I began to pray that the rain would hold off, just until I arrived, so I wouldn't be completely soaked and the Lord said, *"Don't ask Me. You tell it not to rain."*

I was a little incredulous. "You want **me** to tell it not to rain?"

"Command it not to rain until you get to church."

I was thinking I might be a bit too tired but I also knew the voice of God well enough to know that He was serious. I was either going to command the rain or I was going to get drenched. So I did. I looked out the window and told the sky, "You cannot rain until I step foot in the church, then you can rain all you want." I said it with authority even though I felt more than a little silly.

As I finished preparing for church I heard the first drops of rain falling, but, to my surprise, the moment I stepped out the door the rain stopped. It did not start again until seconds after I got under the cover near the front doors of the church.

With very few exceptions, when I didn't think about commanding the rain, I never got stuck walking in the rain in Tampa during my 2 year stay and I did a lot of walking.

I forget this lesson more often than I care to admit, but when I remember it, I also recall that as Jesus is, so are we in this world (1st John 4:17) and if He could speak directly to the wind, waves and storms; then we have that same power and authority as joint-heirs with Him.

It makes me wonder what my life would look like, what the life of the Church would look like, if we actually took His promises seriously and started exercising the same power and authority Jesus demonstrated when He walked the earth. What would it look like if we really understood the precious gift of the indwelling Holy Spirit freely given to us to empower us to do that very thing?

Ask

Knock and it will be opened
Ask and you shall receive
Speak to this mountain
And it must move
If only you believe

Acknowledge Me in all your ways
I will make straight your path
My grace is sufficient for you
You won't fall, you won't turn back

Do not worry or be anxious
Trust Me and be still
Come near again and seek My face
Know My perfect will

Knock and it will be opened
Ask and you shall receive
Speak to this mountain
And it will move
If only you believe

Key: Christ in You

Do you understand the riches of the glory of Christ in you? Do you understand what this really means in your life and your experience in this world?

Meditate on this: **"To whom God WOULD MAKE KNOWN what is the riches of the glory of the mystery among the Gentiles; which is Christ in you, the hope of glory."** *(Colossians 1:27)*

Delve deeper.

"Habitation of God" - to what end? To what purpose?

What riches are yours because Jesus lives continually in you and in Him all the fullness of the Godhead dwells?

Explore this.

Don't leave anything on the table. It ALL belongs to you!

Are you living as if you are My habitation, My literal dwelling place?

Are you living as one who has access to all of My fullness, all the time?

Are you living as a much-loved child; one who is accepted and delighted in by your Father?

Are you living as if you know that it is I Who am working in and through you?

*Beloved, I am mighty **in you**.*

My power is not limited or diminished in the slightest because I abide in you. *My ability is only limited in its manifestation by your knowledge of Me and your willingness to partner with Me in faith and your obedience.*

Know *with absolute certainty that I desire to move, to act, to speak, to show forth My glory and My love and goodness both to you and through you.*

I have given you fullness, riches, abundance, might, strength, peace, love, favor and grace. I AM limitless, infinite, all mighty; nothing is impossible with Me; and you live in Me, as I live in you!

How would your life look different if you lived as if this were true?

How would your life change if Christ in you, the hope of glory, became your daily reality?

I AM limitless, infinite, all mighty; nothing is impossible with Me; and you live in Me as I live in you!

Colossians 1:27

To whom God was pleased to make known how great
for the Gentiles are the riches of the glory of this
mystery, which is Christ within and among you, the
Hope of [realizing the] glory.

Anysia Derora

Singing Freedom Over Me

I am changed
When I hear You call my name
I'm transformed
I'll never be the same
You're calling me higher
Calling me deeper
Calling me nearer
So I can hear Your song

You've opened up my ears to hear
Opened up my heart to receive
The freedom that You're singing over me

I hear You singing freedom
Hear You singing freedom
Hear You singing freedom over me
I hear You singing freedom
Hear You singing freedom
Hear You singing freedom over me

You love me
You draw me
Closer and closer to Your heart
Tell me I'm Your treasure
I'm Your very own reward
And I'm transformed
As I become what I behold
And I behold You
I behold You
Singing over me

I hear You singing freedom
Hear You singing freedom
Hear You singing freedom over me
I hear You singing freedom
Hear You singing freedom
Hear You singing freedom over me

The Lord God, the One who created the universe with the words of His mouth is, right now, singing over you and singing over me. He is exulting over us with song...words and melodies...and I believe each song is unique to the one to whom He sings it.

If His spoken Word created galaxies known and yet undiscovered, – have you ever wondered how much power is contained in the song that He sings over you?

He is creating something, declaring your purpose and His absolute delight in you every moment of every day!

"Singing Freedom Over Me" is a song I wrote acknowledging the song I heard Him singing over me; a reminder that no matter what His song never ends, and, like His Word, never returns to Him void, without accomplishing that for which He sings it!

Nugget: Intimate Invitation

2nd Peter 1:3-4 KJV According to His divine power hath given unto us all things that pertain to life and godliness, through the knowledge of Him that hath called us to glory and virtue. Whereby are given unto us exceeding great and precious promises; that by these ye might be partakers of the divine nature, having escaped the corruption that is in the world through lust.

Jesus Christ, the Messiah, our Savior, Who is perfect in power and never changes has already given to us, the Church, ALL THINGS that pertain to life and godliness...we only need to partake.

God offers us an intimate life with Him, whereby the fullness of His life becomes ours to the degree that we will partake of that life and we partake of that life by knowing Him and surrendering everything to Him.

The more we set ourselves apart unto God, the more we attain to the abundance of life He has given to us.

Is there anything more intimate than pouring your own life into another? I think of a baby nursing on his mother's breast - her life flowing into her child. There is a bond that forms as the life of one flows into the other, giving life and sustenance - **all things** pertaining to life for that baby are coming from the mother.

In much the same way, Jesus invites us to partake of His life, to be sustained by His very life, to enter into intimate fellowship with Him; drinking deeply of His person, of His Word, of His presence. He invites us to be filled and quickened, overflowing with His Spirit, which is His life.

We can drink our fill at the never drying well of Jesus. We can eat our fill of Him through His Word. We can partake of pure, intimate fellowship with our God and Savior and in so doing become more and more like Him, for surely as we behold Him we become like Him.

Beloved, the Lord has given to us everything we need, the only question is - will we partake or will we leave what He has freely given to us on the table, untouched, un-enjoyed, unexperienced?

Storms

I've been running in fear, trying to hide
From the storm raging in my heart
But a whisper is rising, reminding me
I don't have to fall apart

I am healed. I am whole. I am redeemed.
I am a chosen child of the King
I am strong. I am stable. I am secure.
I find rest in His perfect love for me.

I will not be moved!
I will not be overcome!
I will stand; I will prevail!
I will rise above.

Running to our secret place,
held safely in His arms
I find the refuge I've been seeking
to take me through these storms.

Key: Permission

You have permission to be who I called you to be. You have permission to be good, kind, encouraging and vibrantly alive.

You have permission to be bold, wise, gentle and strong in Me and the power of My might. You have permission to rest and flow with My Spirit within you. What you have heard is absolutely correct, surely you choose the level to which you will rise in Me!

Beloved, I have never been afraid of you getting too far ahead of Me. There is nowhere you can go that I am not. Do you think that I am unable to arrest your attention if you're not prepared for the place you are stepping into?

I delight in your enthusiasm and desire to know Me and to explore the endless expanse of My precious promises! I enjoy watching you dig deeper, believe more radically in My Word and thrill at each discovery!

Yes! Explore Me!

Yes! Come deeper! Plumb My depths.

Dare to believe Me for greater, for better, for more. My Kingdom and all it contains is set before you. An immeasurable territory of promise, abundance and life is at your feet and all you have to do is step in.

You don't have to be tentative! It is My delight to give you the Kingdom! Enter in! Enjoy! Delight! Explore! Ask! Listen! Receive! Occupy!
You have My permission. I release you to be fully Mine, fully who I created you to be.

Burn brightly! Shine! Be My love song to the world! Be My living love letter!

Call to mind who I AM - the unlimited, all-powerful, all-seeing, all-knowing Creator of the Universe and, as you keep this in mind, recall that you are in Me and I am in you therefore you are limitless in Me!

Only believe!

Nothing will be impossible for the one who dares to believe I am Who I am.

Dare to believe! Have the holy audacity to take Me at My Word.

You have My permission to partake of My fullness and of all you receive, to freely and liberally pour it back into the lives of others. Pour out My love, My favor, My kindness, My mercy, My goodness, My forgiveness, My liberty and watch as I bless others through you, through your words, through your touch, through your prayers, through your worship - and change the entire landscape of your life and the lives of those around you!

How deep do you want to go?

How brightly do you want to shine?

How much do you want to explore?

It's all yours!

Lay hold and do not shrink back!

This is My delight. Enjoy it with Me. Partake of what I have made you a partaker of.

Enjoy My lavish liberality and share it with others...then watch everything change!

Watch mountains crumble, obstacles move; doors open!

Enter into My fullness and My favor and see what I will do on behalf of those whose hearts are set on Me."

How deep do you want to go?

How brightly do you want to shine?

How much do you want to explore?

It's ALL yours!

Lay hold and do not shrink back!

Holy Spirit Rain

Holy Spirit rain
Come wash away
The masks
The person
I have tried
In vain
To be

Erode the walls
Disarm me
I surrender
See the flag
My towers
Are not the places
I belong
Here I am God
My passions
My dreams
All my desires
The things
I put aside
To be the person
I thought
You required

Holy Spirit rain
Come wash me clean
Of all the things
I've tried so hard
To be

Here I am
A woman
A daughter
A child
Free me
From the prison
These hands built

Let me
Find myself in You
Let me
Worship You
In truth
I surrender all
God here I am
Holy Spirit
Sweet, sweet Spirit
Rain

Nugget: The Wilderness of the Heart

Isaiah 35:1 The wilderness and the dry land shall be glad; the desert shall rejoice and blossom like the rose and the autumn crocus

*T*he scary, dangerous, untamed, unmapped, hazardous, lonely, isolated, fear-filled places in our hearts, minds and lives shall be glad!

There are places in my mind and emotions fraught with peril, landmines, booby traps and crawling with creatures that prey on peace, joy, contentment and patience. These "creatures" are not demons but lies from the past, limiting beliefs, warped perceptions, wrong lenses and ways of understanding, worldly definitions applied to Kingdom principles.

The danger is in becoming beguiled by them and falling into the despair of their lairs. There are tricks and triggers to be aware of and knowing these can help navigate them for a time but if our minds and emotions are to become fruitful and flourishing places to travel then they must be transformed. The viper pits and cesspools of lies must be utterly eradicated. A relentless battle must be waged to turn these danger zones into delight zones; and wastelands of doubt and unbelief into fertile, blossoming valleys of faith, fragrant with life and wonder.

This is not a passive process. This is an intentional removal of the giants from the habitation of the landscape of our lives and a deliberate possession of this precious inner territory and it begins by agreeing with the Word of God and reckoning ourselves dead to sin, but alive to righteousness. It is the purpose-filled action of daily, sometimes hourly, putting off the old, and putting on the new.

When we determine to forget all that lies behind and let the old, sin-laden person of the past remain buried with Christ; we can begin to align ourselves with the truth that we are new creations; leave behind the chains which He destroyed and live a life of promise, vibrantly alive and flourishing as we allow God Himself to reveal who we are.

A relentless battle must be waged

to turn these danger zones into

delight zones;

and wastelands of doubt and unbelief,

into fertile, blossoming

valleys of faith;

fragrant with life and wonder.

I See the Lord

I see the Lord
He's calling out to me
but I am sitting in this boat
and He's walking on the sea

I hear Him calling out my name
I leap – then see the storm
my mind, it screams, "IMPOSSIBLE"
but my heart longs for His arms

And I cry "Lord, Lord,
please tell me what to do."
He said *"Step out of the boat, child,
no harm will come to you"*

At His word I forget the world
and stand up on my feet,
the storm is still there raging,
I can feel my own heart beat

But straight ahead I see my Lord
waiting there for me
so I breathe deep and look at Him
and step out on the sea

And I cry "Lord, Lord,
please tell me what to do."
He said *"Keep your eyes on Me, child,
no harm will come to you"*

So I leave behind the little boat
and take a step of faith
keeping my eyes on Jesus
letting the waters rage

Drawing ever nearer
He takes my hand in His
and says *"My child, you were born
for such a time as this."*

And I cry "Lord, Lord
please tell me what to do."
He says *"Be a willing vessel
and I will live through you"*

Since then there have still been times
I've turned my eyes away
but as I sink, He lifts me up
and I can hear Him say

*"Child I am with you
no matter what you do
and in your moment of despair
know I am there with you*

*If you will be still and listen
you'll hear My voice break through
saying "Child here am I –
look to Me, I am still with you."*

And in those times I'm learning
that if I look beyond the storm
I will not just see the trouble
but I will see the Lord.

Nugget: Promises

One morning, in that place between dream and sleep the Lord asked me a question, *"Do you know where you're heading?"* followed immediately by, *"Don't forget to take your promises with you."*

When I woke up He said to me, *"This redirect was My plan. Don't worry. I know where we're going and it's going to be better than you can imagine. There are promises I've given you for this time and this season - take them out, dig in, ask Me about them. You'll need them on this journey."*

This is true of all of us. God gives us promises for the journey. He loves to make promises and He loves even more to keep those promises. He gives us promises in scripture, promises in prophetic words, promises in dreams and in our communion with Him and all of those promises He is intent upon keeping. In fact, He wants our lives to be living testimonies to the fact that He is upright and faithful to keep His promises.

Psalm 92:15 [They are living memorials] to show that the Lord is upright and faithful to His promises; He is my Rock, and there is no unrighteousness in Him.

What promises has God given you for just this time and season in your life? What are you doing with them?

Always Be Enough

I come to the shores of Your ocean
You bid me to come in.
And in the healing waters
You cleanse me of my sin.

Your grace and mercy lift the pain
and leave it on the shore.
I look…part of me is missing….
You say it's part of me no more.

In the water Your love surrounds me
still, I think of all I've done….
by Your loving-kindness You remind me
"I see you through My Son."

"Oh, precious daughter, you are Mine,
these waters are for you.
The banks of the world are cluttered with lies;
come drink of what is true."

"Live and play in the ocean of My love,
you are My delight.
You never have to leave again,
for herein is your life."

"Let My Spirit fill you.
Let My fullness heal your heart.
Let My presence be your breath.
Remain in Me – be set apart."

"I am everything you need,
dear child, you are Mine.
All I have – I give to you.
Come taste this love divine.

"Do not fear the storms
or dread the ever changing sea
for I am ever constant,
daily drawing you to Me."

"I alone am your fullness
and you are My desire.
Don't linger on the shore – jump in
let Me change you with My fire."

"I and I alone know
your every thought and deed.
I am your Lord and your Provider,
I alone am what you need."

"Leave the shores of the world behind,
come into My love.
I am everything you need
and I will always be enough."

I wrote **"Always be Enough"** in April of 1998 in Cannon Beach as I tried to capture the amazing things God was speaking to my heart.

More than 18 years later, I still return to the promise in these words of truth and comfort. Time and again this promise, that God will, indeed, always be enough, echoes in my heart and strengthens me to keep going deeper in my relationship with Him.

Sea of Glass

I have bled on the sea of glass
Spread out before Your throne
Years of death and dying
Others have never seen or known
But You do see and You do know
And still You bid me come
You stretch out Your hand
Unafraid to touch
What others cannot, will not see
What they cannot accept
You embrace and heal and love
Bringing life from death

I have stood before Your throne
Blood flowing from wounds unseen
Ashamed to bleed in such a place
So beautiful, pure and clean
But You tell me this is our place
The place where I can heal
Where I don't have to hide the hurt
Where I can just be real

I'm hurting God, all over
Overtaken by the pain
I cannot see my hand before me
Through this driving rain
You are sure, You won't let me fall
You won't let me drown
Help me breathe, hold me again
You won't let me down

Winter will not last forever
This death cannot remain
The heaviness and darkness
Must move on with the rain
Only Your Word will stand unmoved
You are all that's true
And I can rest in Your sure promise
That You make all things new

God is not afraid or ashamed of the wounds we bear. He loves it when we come to Him in times of vulnerability, fear, dismay or grief to take refuge in His arms. He joyfully welcomes the weak and the weary.

"Sea of Glass" was written during a time in my life, when it seemed that all that could be shaken was.

I tried repeatedly to be strong in my own strength but didn't ever find rest and healing until I set my unrealistic expectations of myself aside and came, in all my brokenness and mess to the throne of God.

Time and again He met me there, never once frustrated, always gentle – and in that place of humility He restored my soul, though I could do nothing for myself.

Key: Ask

The abundant life is a life of power! It is a life of confidence! It is a life of victory over all the works of the devil and all the curse of the law! It is a life without want, for all you have need of is in My presence! It is a life of dominion: a life filled with the glory of My presence through the indwelling of My Spirit!

You are indwelt by My Spirit! The Spirit of the Most High God! The same Spirit Who led and empowered Jesus, leads and empowers you! Not a lesser spirit with less power - the very same Holy Spirit! Know with confident assurance that nothing, no nothing, is impossible for you if you will steadfastly believe and refuse to waiver.

What do you have need of?

Ask and believe you have received it, knowing I hear your requests. Speak forth the desires of your heart – nothing is too big or too difficult for Me! There is no limit to My power! Likewise, nothing is so small as to be beneath Me! Oh that you would ask and allow Me to move on your behalf. I desire to bless you! I desire to be involved in every area of your life, if only you would ask.

Hold nothing back as you commune with Me. You are precious to Me. You are My Beloved. I will withhold nothing from you. I long to shower you with gifts, with the desires of your heart but most of all with My presence. Oh My Bride, My beautiful, beloved Bride, I long to give all of Myself to you. I desire you with fiery passion that will not be denied. I long to reveal Myself to you if only you would desire Me and set your whole heart on Me.

There are those who will never know the beauty of intimacy with Me as long as they are on earth because the world holds their attention far more than I do. But this is not My will!

*I will that you would know My passion, My presence, My glory, My power, here, today, in this life! **That** is the abundant life I came to give you. A life united to Me, a life saturated and consumed by love. This is the place of My glory and it is available to you here; it is available to you now.*

You are indwelt by My Spirit!

The Spirit of the Most High God!

The same Spirit Who led and

empowered Jesus;

leads and empowers you!

Guide My Path

All the days of my life
are written in Your book
nothing catches You unaware
From beginning to end
You've numbered my days
so nothing can cause me to fear

        Because You guide my path
        You light my way
        You direct every step
        That I faithfully take

        You're my light in the darkness
        My song in the night
        My passion, my peace
        And my life

You know what I don't know
You see what I can't see
Your understanding far exceeds mine
You bid me to come,
Cease striving and know
I am Yours, and I'll be just fine

        Because You guide my path
        You light my way
        You direct every step
        That I faithfully take

        You're my light in the darkness
        My song in the night
        My passion, my peace
        And my life

Words

You answer me by fire
From the secret place of thunder
You are God
And You answer me

You draw me nearer
to reveal
The truth of all creation
There is power
In every word I speak

Every song I sing
Every prayer I pray
You remind me
That every word can be

Clothed in fire
Wrapped in thunder
Born of the awe and wonder
The wonder of the secret place of God

To set the captive free
To heal the broken heart
To restore the wounded
Redeem the lost
Reveal the glory of Who You are

As it is in heaven
Let it be
Here in this earth
As we release

Words of fire
Wrapped in thunder
Born of the awe and wonder
The wonder of the secret place of God

You answer me by fire
From the secret place of thunder
You are God
And You answer me
You are God
And You answer me

Key: Come Know Me

*M*emorizing **"For with God nothing shall be impossible"** *is good. You could go your whole life performing signs, wonders and miracles based solely on your faith in the truth of that verse; but you would not know Me. You would not fulfill your destiny. You would live a shell of a life full of the praise and accolades of men but completely desolate in your inner man. Like Israel, you would only know something about My works but you would not know My heart. I have created you to discover My heart, My motives, My ways; to truly know Me and to walk in unbroken communion with Me.*

*Too many people approach Me like they do a movie star or famous person - they read **about** Me; hear **about** Me and can even talk **about** Me for hours but it's all hear-say; external and shallow. They do not know Me.*

Oh, that My people would know Me. That they would know My heart and enjoy My presence. But they are content with a second-hand Christianity that appeals to their soul but never truly touches their spirit. They are content knowing about Me when I created them to know Me and then they wonder why their experience looks so different from their heroes of faith - so void of My real presence, power, love, and provision.

Created for intimacy they setting for a 30-minute sermon once a week, or less.

I want them to esteem Me worthy of taking the time to get to know; worthy of seeking; worthy of listening to; worthy of their attention, affection and adoration.

Do you realize, Beloved, that none of the people you admire in the Bible had a Bible as you know it today? What did they have instead? Enoch had Me. Noah had Me. Abraham had Me. Isaac and Jacob had Me. Joseph had Me. Moses, Joshua and Caleb had Me. Peter and Paul had Me. They journeyed with Me and got to know Me along the way, listening to My voice, making mistakes, correcting their course and continually drawing near to Me.

I am not undermining My written Word; I gave it to you for a reason! The Bible is My idea. I want the Body to have it as a living love letter illustrating My character, My nature, My boundless love for those who call on My Name. I want the Word to remind My people that I am God of the impossible. It is an invitation, a foretaste, living and powerful and yet not a substitute for the vibrant and vital relationship I desire you to have with Me.

I want to teach you to abide in Me always. I want to reveal My heart to you. I want you and I to have such an intimate and beautiful relationship that others desire to know Me as you do.

I love you. You are My bride. Let us get to know one another as friends and lovers as we journey together, hand in hand and heart to heart. Come, know Me!

I have created you to discover
My heart, My motives, My ways;
to truly know Me
and to walk in
unbroken communion with Me.

Growing Up

Abba Papa – I see Your hands
just a finger stretch away
I hear Your voice urging me forward –
telling me not to stay.

My balance is not so good
but I hear You call
and I take a step toward You
trusting You won't let me fall.

One step forward, wobbling,
You take a small step back.
I stretch, but You urge me on
I smile, I hear You laugh.

For just a moment I pause,
You're still so very near;
I am overwhelmed with desire,
drowning any fear.

Each step I take, it seems so small
but I must reach Your hands.
I start to fall – You right me
and we start again.

Every step I take – You smile –
it's not so small to You.
You know how much I want to run,
You see me trying to.

Still I hear Your soothing voice
saying *"It's O.K.,*
running will come soon enough,
learn to walk today."

"Be content that you are learning
that you know I am here
and I will meet your yearning
as you run with confidence, not fear."

*"Learn to walk in the safety
of the abundance of My love
and know each step is just
another part of growing up."*

Every step I take –

You smile –

It's not so small to You!

Testimony: The Apple

I was in Tampa, Florida to finish Bible School. The whole move was a step of faith and obedience. All my needs were met time and time again. In this midst of oh so many miracles, this one stands out to me as a continual reminder of amazing faithfulness of God to hear us and to care about the "little" things.

At the time I didn't have a car and I worked a little over a mile from school, so God and I had some wonderful talks on my walk. I didn't have a lot of money. I was really living off of stuff I could buy in a vending machine, things people gave me and Top Ramen; which was totally fine with me because I was also seeing God's incredible faithfulness day after day.

On this particular day, I just casually mentioned that I would really like an apple. It wasn't a request exactly, just mentioning a craving to my Father.

When I arrived at school, one of my new friends walked up to me and said that as she was leaving the house, the lady she was renting a room from gave her a couple apples. She had told her that she really would only eat one but the lady insisted that she take both.

As soon as the lady insisted, my friend thought of me. And there she was, standing in front of me offering me an apple, less than 20 minutes after I had told Papa that I wanted one.

I was in tears and I realized how incredible the heart of God was to provide for me. It may have seemed insignificant to anyone else, but to my heart it declared with absolute certainty that He cared enough to make provision for a desire of my heart before I ever mentioned it to Him.

Psalm 139:4

For there is not a word in my tongue
[still unuttered], but, behold,
O Lord, You know it altogether.

You Are Mine

You are My well-beloved
Walking in My grace
Enfolded in My loving arms
Ever before My face

I will not leave you or forsake you
You and I are one
I delight in who you are today
And in who you will become

Do not fear, for I am with You
Your shield, strength and song
You are My well-loved child
Drink deeply of My love

Let Me heal you
Let Me fill you
Let My love overflow
So all who see will know
That you are Mine
You are Mine

Nugget: Nothing Insignificant

*T*he Holy Spirit is a genius!

One morning I told Him I was missing a friend and that even though they weren't in a place we could talk, I just wanted to hear their voice. I was not expecting an answer. I was just sharing my heart. But guess what?! He is the God who hears and cares, even about seemingly simple, insignificant things! And He gently reminded me that I could just put on one of their CDs and hear their voice as much as I wanted! (Perhaps this is why I am blessed to know so many musicians, singers and teachers?)

Sometimes we believe that God is too big or too busy to care about the little things that mean a lot to us, so we don't ask. We may even rationalize that others have bigger, more important things they need from Him so "I don't want to bother Him." And in doing that we forget...**He is God**!

He is unlimited. He is not bound by time or to-do lists that are too long already. His calendar is not full. He doesn't have somewhere more important to be than with you. **He doesn't have anything or anyone more pressing on His heart or mind than you.**

You cannot in any way diminish His power and availability in the life of someone else just because you need Him! He loves when we share the whole of our lives and hearts with us. He delights in answering and lavishing us in His presence. Yes, He's that big, that good, that crazy about you!

He is unlimited.

He is not bound by time

or to-do lists

that are too long already!

His calendar is not full!

He doesn't have somewhere

more important to be

than with you!

You Welcomed Me

You welcomed me
You waited for me
Indescribable gifts in Your hands
Healing, salvation,
a love that's not based on
anything I could do
You made all things new
When, You welcomed me

You knew I would come
You set Your heart on me
Your love kept calling my name
And when I answered
How You rejoiced
And left me forever changed

You welcomed me
You waited for me
Indescribable gifts in Your hands
Healing, salvation,
a love that's not based on
anything I could do
You made all things new
When, You welcomed me

Each day is a new gift
Wrapped in Your love
Immersed in Your presence
and grace
Oh how amazing
knowing that daily
I walk on the light
of Your ways

You welcomed me
You waited for me
Indescribable gifts in Your hands
Healing, salvation,
a love that's not based on
anything I could do
You made all things new
When, You welcomed me

I wrote the chorus to **"You Welcomed Me"** at a conference for Worship Leaders where Paul Baloche, Kathryn Scott and Brian Doerekson were speaking.

One of the segments Paul Baloche was talking about how often he writes songs for things he sees. He said that one of the things he had never written a song about was that moment in the airport when the person sees those who are waiting for them. The quickened step, the gifts, the love, the laughter, and the delight.

As I sat listening to him, I could picture God as the one waiting for me at the airport as a picture of salvation; and all the gifts, love, joy and delight he has in store for each one who turns to Him. This song is a part of His invitation to not lean on our own understanding but to trust His love and His direction for us.

Nugget: Choosing Your Filter

*E*veryone survives something. We all go through things – things we experience at the hands of others or ourselves; things we experience as a result of our own choices and through no choice of our own. It's a reality of life.

From conception we begin to create filters based on input, based on experience and these filters change and expand as we do. Our filters tell us what is right and wrong and they govern how we interpret every circumstance and situation; shading how we view other people, ourselves and the things we experience. A filter impacts not only **what** we hear, see and feel but **how** we hear, see and feel.

One person may walk into a new situation with new people energized, excited and ready to light up the room; another may be terrified with their mind racing through all the possible scenarios they might encounter and how they should react in each one. One may be looking for the center of the room and how they can speak to every person possible and another is looking for a space close to an exit where they might go unnoticed and easily slip out. This is partly personality and partly filter.

The beauty of filters is that they can change. The biggest hindrance to changing our filters is understanding that we have them and that they may, in fact, be wrong, skewed or tainted.

Once we come to understand that our perceptions can be changed we enter into a place of tremendous power in our lives – power because we suddenly give ourselves the ability to change our minds and our lives. A whole new landscape appears before us the moment we open ourselves up to the reality of choice.

If you've ever worn glasses, you're probably familiar with the process. You first get your glasses and it's like seeing the world clearly for the first time; everything is fresh and crisp. You can't believe all you've been missing. Eventually your eyes adjust and you don't even notice that you are missing things again. Then you go back for your eye exam and get an upgraded prescription and you experience that sharp clarity once again and wonder that you didn't realize just how much you needed a new prescription.

The same is true with the filters through which we view life. We can always use an updated prescription. This is why Romans 12:2 says: **Do not be conformed to this world (this age), [fashioned after and adapted to its external, superficial customs], but be transformed (changed) by the [entire] renewal of your mind [by its new ideals and its new attitude], so that you may prove [for yourselves] what is the good and acceptable and perfect will of God, even the thing which is good and acceptable and perfect [in His sight for you].**

By our filters we either conform to the world around us and remain bound to the past – good, bad and otherwise; or we find ourselves transformed to see from a Kingdom perspective through the mind of Christ that is given to us the moment we accept His sacrifice on our behalf and begin to walk with Him.

We have a perpetual invitation to raise our expectations to the level of God's; to see things from a higher place; to understand in light of God's perfect love and perfect knowledge.

It's a process. Day by day we can experience a new upgrade in how we see things, understand them and interpret them. Day by day we can lay our old filter at the foot of the throne and take up God's perspective, learning to walk in that instead of how we've always walked.

We literally have the opportunity to choose to remain captive to the past, identified by how the world tried to mold and shape us, or to choose the freedom of being defined instead by God and His perfect love.

We can live a life of continually increasing clarity in the light of Who God is in us, to us and for us and who we are in Him or we can say, "this is just who I am and it's just the way it is" and remain confined in the prison of a way of seeing and thinking that only allows us to live life as far as the chains of our un-renewed minds permit.

The world would like to tell us that there are some things that simply cannot be changed; some damage that cannot be reversed; some defense mechanisms and ways of viewing life that will remain unaltered because of how deeply rooted they are in our personal experiences – but that is not what God says!

We can choose to renew our minds with the Word of God and in wonderful personal time with Him; and in the process find that absolutely everything is subject to change when the Unchanging God is moving on our behalf.

...absolutely everything
is subject to change
when the unchanging God
is moving on our behalf.

You Captivate Me

My heart is overwhelmed, Lord
So I choose to lift my eyes
To the mountains You created
And the rainbow in the sky

I know You're with me, You love me
You're my refuge in the storm
So I come into Your presence
And take solace in Your arms

I rest my head upon Your chest
Breathe in the song You sing
Such peace I find in knowing
That Your heart is holding me

Lord, You captivate me
There is no one else like You
You still my trembling heart
and catch my tears

Lord, You captivate me
You're my refuge and my strength
when the dreams I hold
can't hold me
You are there

My heart is overwhelmed, Lord
So I choose to lift my eyes
To the mountains You created
And the rainbow in the sky

I know You're with me, You love me
You're my refuge in the storm
So I come into Your presence
And take solace in Your arms

Exodus 34:29-30

When Moses came down from Mount Sinai with the two tables of the Testimony in his hand, he did not know that the skin of his face shone *and* sent forth beams by reason of his speaking with the Lord. When Aaron and all the Israelites saw Moses, behold, the skin of his face shone, and they feared to come near him.

Arise, Shine

Arise, shine
for the glory of the Lord is upon you
and that glory is the light that shines
in all you say and do

As darkness overtakes the earth
upon you the Lord will rise
can't you hear Him calling you –
saying "Child, arise and shine."

For the mountains may be removed
the hills may shake and tremble
but God goes before and behind
you will not fall or stumble

His covenant of love still stands
His peace cannot be taken
He stands at your right hand
you will not be shaken

The devil, he may prowl around
his lies to loudly roar
but he is far beneath your feet
an eternally defeated foe

So arise, shine
for the glory of the Lord is upon you
and that glory is the light that shines
in all you say and all you do

As darkness overtakes the earth
upon you the Lord will rise
can't you hear Him calling you –
saying "Child, arise and shine."

Nugget: Acts of Worship

Your decision to not worry or fret but to dance, laugh, sing and enjoy every moment is, in and of itself, a profound act of worship!

Every joyful spin, every delighted step declares to all that you trust in the Lord your God, Who cannot and will not fail. You are His and you can rest beneath the wildly waving victory banner of His perfect love for you!

You can choose, with great intentionality, to worship Him with your delight in this life and unwavering confidence that He withholds no good thing from you! After all, how will He who did not withhold His Own Son from you but gave Him freely, not also, with Him, freely give you all things?

So go ahead...let the laughter bubble up, play, dance, sing, skip, enjoy this moment, knowing God, your God, is joining in with you.

**You are His
and you can rest
beneath the wildly waving banner
of His perfect love for you.**

Scars that Set Me Free

You left Your throne in heaven
Laid Your glory down
Set aside Your royal robes
To wear a thorn knit crown

You left the angels adoration
Creator made creation
Born to pass the greatest test
My God who put on human flesh

You became
Unrecognizable for me

      Unrecognizable as the man You came to be
      You still bear the scars that set me free
      Beauty and perfection meet
      In Your blood that flows from Calvary
      And I am healed while You still bear
      The scars that set me free

You came to live so You could die
In humility be crucified
You bore my sin, You bore my shame
Willingly You were disgraced

The wounds You bore
You bore for me
Your dying breath
My victory

You became
Unrecognizable for me

      Unrecognizable as the man You came to be
      You still bear the scars that set me free
      Beauty and perfection meet
      In Your blood that flows from Calvary
      And I am healed while You still bear
      The scars that set me free
      I am healed while You still bear
      The scars that set me free

I've had on-again-off-again struggles with self-injury since High School. Sometimes I've even had years between incidents, years without it even being a passing thought.

The song **"Scars that Set Me Free"** is one I wrote during a time when I was actively hurting myself after a conversation with the Lord, where He reminded me that, while my scars are real, they are also temporary and the scars Jesus currently bears are eternal and were borne on my behalf. He bled for me, so I don't have to.

This isn't something I always remember when I feel like I'm drowning in an unstoppable tsunami of stress, pain and intense emotions from the past, but when I do remember, I find tremendous comfort in knowing that I have a High Priest Who is touched, in every sense of the word, by my own weakness, pain and distress, and Who desires for me to remember He has already carried it all on my behalf – with Love and understanding beyond expression.

Isaiah 53: 4-5

Surely He has borne our griefs (sicknesses, weaknesses, and distresses) and carried our sorrows and pains [of punishment], yet we [ignorantly] considered Him stricken, smitten, and afflicted by God [as if with leprosy]. But He was wounded for our transgressions, He was bruised for our guilt and iniquities; the chastisement [needful to obtain] peace and well-being for us was upon Him, and with the stripes [that wounded] Him we are healed and made whole.

Laugh

I laugh at destruction and famine
I laugh as one who can't see
and the Lord God Almighty
seated in Heaven
joins in and laughs with me

Don't look at my circumstances
or the storm I seem to be in
Jesus Christ is my victory
and I always triumph through Him!

So I laugh at destruction and famine
I laugh as one who can't see
and the Lord God Almighty
seated in Heaven
joins in and laughs with me

Like my King and my Creator
I speak forth what eye cannot see
and believing I call into being
all He has promised me

So I don't look at my circumstances
or the storm I seem to be in
For Jesus Christ is my victory
and I always triumph through Him!

That's why I laugh at destruction and famine
Yes, I laugh as one who can't see
And the Lord God Almighty
seated in Heaven
Joins in and laughs with me
oh, the Lord God almighty
seated in heaven
joins in and laughs with me

Job 5:22 At destruction and famine you shall laugh, neither shall you be afraid of the living creatures of the earth.

When the Lord sent me to finish Bible School in 2005 it was a tremendous exercise in faith. There were so many occasions when I didn't know how God was going to come through and I held fast to His promise that He would provide because I'm worth more to Him than many sparrows.

The night I wrote "Laugh" my faith was shaken. I was in class, frustrated and tired of not knowing in advance where and how my needs were going to be met. My instructor referenced Job 5:22 in his teaching and the song flood my soul and filled me with renewed hope, that I could trust the Lord and I could laugh with God in the face of the enemy who was trying to distract me from God's unceasing provision in my life.

Enough

Behold, I stand here waiting
to give you all of Me,
to be your Strength in weakness,
your Provider in time of need.

I gave My Son so you could know
the fullness of My love,
so I could fill you with Myself.
For you – I will be enough.

Behold, I stand here longing
to be your heart's desire,
to be the One you come to,
to ignite you with My fire.

I want to wrap you in My presence,
to shower you with love
to show My awesome power,
for you to know I am enough.

Behold, I stand here calling
I know you by heart, by name,
come to Me, I'm waiting -
you will never be the same.

I long to move upon you,
for you to know My will,
to quiet you in My love
and whisper when you're still.

Do you hear Me calling?
Hear the longing in My voice?
Do you feel My desire?
Do you know you are My choice?

Behold I stand here waiting
with passion, grace and love.
Come to Me and see I'm faithful
and I will always be enough.

Key: Fearless Love

I love you!

I don't care if you make mistakes, stumble, fall or even completely crash. I am utterly unconcerned about your shortcomings and the mistakes that you have made or will make along the way.

I am with you!

I am the One Who made you daring, fearless, passionate, bold and endlessly curious. When you leap, My arms are ready and willing to catch you. When you stumble, My hands will lift you up and dust you off.

Beloved, what if it's true?

What if My ceaseless, unconditional love for you is the only safety net you have and the only safety net you need?

What if you knew you could give something your all and lose without fear of condemnation or criticism?

What if you believed you could come to Me muddy, bruised and covered with blood, sweat and tears from the effort and be met with My embrace, delight and pleasure?

The certainty of My love truly makes your life risk free; for I will not change towards you.

I love the process you are engaged in and the enthusiasm with which you approach it, even when that enthusiasm means you make mistakes.

Child, My love bears up under any and all things. I know the end from the beginning and am never surprised by what happens in your life. I've gone before you. I've made the rough places smooth.

Only believe and enjoy this journey into audacious faith and fearless love.

The certainty of My love
truly makes your life risk free,
for I will not change towards you!

1st Corinthians 13:7

Love bears up under anything and everything
that comes, is ever ready to believe the best of
every person, its hopes are fadeless under all
circumstances, and it endures everything
[without weakening].

Broken Bread, Poured Out Wine

Come to Me just as you are.
I'll give you beauty for your ashes,
keep every tear here in this jar.
I love you, My beloved,
precious child of Mine.
You're the reason I became
broken bread and poured out wine.

I've seen everything you've done,
seen how hard you try
to earn the love I give you freely;
to be your own sacrifice.
I have made you clean.
I have set you free.
All you have to do
is believe
and

Come to Me just as you are.
I'll give you beauty for your ashes,
keep every tear here in this jar.
I love you, My beloved,
precious child of Mine.
You're the reason I became
broken bread and poured out wine.

I wrote the song **"Broken Bread, Poured Out Wine"** in Tampa, FL in 2006. I was struggling with my identity and my worth and as I prayed and sought the Lord, trying to lay hold of His truth and His heart for me, I heard Him singing this song over me again and again.

It reminds me that He who knows the true value of all things, esteemed me priceless in His eyes as He hung and bled on the cross to make me His own. He knows what it is to be broken unjustly; to be shamed and ridiculed; to be abandoned; to be alone and He is a High Priest who is personally acquainted with every part of my life – the good, the bad and the ugly – and shares in it all, in ways that are beyond my own comprehension.

Hebrews 4:15 For we do not have a High Priest Who is unable to understand and sympathize and have a shared feeling with our weaknesses and infirmities and liability to the assaults of temptation, but One Who has been tempted in every respect as we are, yet without sinning.

In Your Presence

In Your Presence colors dance
Music comes alive
Your breath electrifies the atmosphere
You take me in Your arms
Bathed in sheer delight
Quieting my soul
with songs of love by night
You hear
You see
And I know that You know
The words that I can't speak
You chase
my every fear
You adorn me in Your love

And You whisper, *"I am here*
And you are Mine.
Come dance in the color
Sing as the music comes alive
As My breath electrifies the atmosphere.
Know I am here.
I am here.
I am with you.
I uphold you.
Come dance and sing
Come lose yourself in praise.
I hear.
I see
I know your heart
I know the words that you can't speak.
For you are Mine."

Nugget: Remodeling the Wilderness

*H*ave you ever described the mountain top experiences of life as the moments of greatest joy, perspective, revelation and victory; the place most desirable to live life from but not the easiest to attain or maintain? Have you ever described the wilderness as a dry, wasteland of testing, trial and loneliness that we must do everything we can to escape so we can start climbing the mountain again and get back to the top of the mountain where everything is okay? I certainly have.

But, what if it's not true?

What if our journey through life with God is, in reality, a vast landscape, varied, unique and beautiful? What if our entire journey with Him contains wonder, majesty and splendor just waiting to be discovered and experienced?

What if the wilderness is just as full of joy, perspective, revelation and victory as the mountaintop but we have been trained by religion and tradition not to even look for it? And what if that is one of the ways the enemy comes into our lives to steal something that is precious to God, something He wants us to have and experience?

Is it possible that the reason the enemy wants you to focus on getting out of the wilderness as quickly as possible is because there is a tremendous wealth of promise and encounter; splendor and glory in that place and he is hoping you just see it as dry, arid and worthless?

Is it possible that he wants to steal from you a substantial territory that God wants you to establish and inhabit with joy and delight?

Some of the greatest revelations of the personality and character of God recorded in the Bible were made in wilderness places. Time and again, when all the person really wanted was resolution – God met them in the wilderness with revelation and everything changed in that place of encounter.

And if the wilderness is never God's will for us then why did the Holy Spirit lead Jesus to the wilderness after His baptism? How can we say the wilderness is a sign of God's displeasure when the Spirit led Jesus there right after the Father had expressed great pleasure in Him ("This is My Beloved Son in Whom I am well-pleased.")? Even after the initial wilderness experience, Jesus spent a good deal of time in the wilderness in prayer, fellowship and ministry.

Is it possible that we can flourish in the wilderness and instead of busting through it like the world and the enemy tells us we should do – we can actually bear great fruit to the glory and honor of God in that place?

Can we be oasis bearers – carrying the oasis of the presence of God into the desert places of life and changing them into places of life, healing, restoration and tremendous beauty?

Are there treasures, promises, encounters awaiting us in the desert that we've bypassed because we didn't slow down to consider that the God who promised to never leave us and never forsake us is actually right there with us and if He is there than anything could happen?

What if the wilderness is a place of wide open space waiting to be explored?

What if it is an invitation into limitless possibilities and tremendous promise? What if the wilderness is the place of vision, dreaming and equipping – a place to be longed for and looked forward to, where only the water of His presence will satisfy and it just so happens to be the only water available?

Isaiah 35 is one of my inheritance scriptures, a precious promise that the Lord gave me in 1998 and I'm still getting fresh revelation from it. Look at the first two verses: **The wilderness and the dry land shall be glad; the desert shall rejoice and blossom like the rose and the autumn crocus. It shall blossom abundantly and rejoice even with joy and singing. The glory of Lebanon shall be given to it, the excellency of [Mount] Carmel and [the plain] of Sharon. They shall see the glory of the Lord, the majesty and splendor and excellency of our God.**

It looks to me like those who belong to God should walk into the wilderness with great anticipation; allowing rivers of living water to flow from us, expecting a place of rejoicing, thanksgiving and encounter which overwhelms all who look at our lives by the revelation of the glory, majesty, splendor and excellency of our God!

If you've been in a wilderness place in your life and you're looking around, praying for rescue and wondering why God seems to be ignoring you, I pray that the eyes of your understanding would be opened and that these words would encourage you to take in a new horizon, to see the landscape around you through a different lens.

Look for your place of encounter with the Lord. Dance and rejoice in the wide open spaces around you. Expect Him to reveal Himself to you in a way that is powerful and transforming. Allow the sound of everlasting joy to rise from your lips and resound through every crack and crevice of the circumstance and look for the treasures of promises, revelation and relationship.

Allow the Spirit of the Living God to thrill your heart and reveal to you what you haven't seen yet.

Believe that something greater is not only possible, but intended. Instead of an unfruitful place of despair and isolation; open your heart to see the tremendous love, delight and desire of the heart of God to have you to Himself in this place and to lavish you with His presence and with revelation upon glorious revelation of Who He is for you right now. Engage your heart with His to see the possibility, the rich promise and treasure that is all around you; to look for the encounter and revelation of His heart. Drink deeply of His intimate presence in this place and delight yourself in Him as rivers spring forth in the wilderness and streams in the desert changing the landscape everywhere you turn.

Dare to allow His love and presence to remodel the so-called wilderness!

Is it possible that the reason the enemy wants you to focus on getting out of the wilderness as quickly as possible is because there is a tremendous wealth of promise and encounter; splendor and glory in that place and he is hoping you only see it as dry, arid and worthless?

Alabaster Box

There was a time my life was empty,
Dark, meaningless and void
No one cared to look at me
There was no peace, no love, no joy

I wore a harlot's garment
And that's all they saw me as
A woman destined to exist
Forever in her past

Through the walls I built around me
No one saw my pain
They never saw the tears that soaked
My pillow like the rain

They didn't see the reasons
Only the clothes I wore
In secret men would lay with me
In public mock me as a whore

Then one day like any other,
I looked upon the face
Of a Man like no other
A Man who saw my pain

With eyes full of compassion
He looked right through the walls
And I knew in an instant
That somehow He saw it all

And seeing all He did not run
He did not turn away
He took my hand into His own
Without any fear or shame

In the glory of such a Love
All my past became undone
Set free by the power
Of a heart willing to touch

He reached into my very soul
And turned everything around
Where once pain and torment reigned
He made love and joy abound

He gave to me the garment
Of a daughter of The King,
Cleansed me in His righteousness,
Gladly set me free

He called me His virgin daughter
Gave me a future without shame
No longer was I whore, or harlot
Because Jesus called my name

All I was I am no more,
Because of Him I live,
And here He is before me
Now is my turn to give.

I find the alabaster box
I've kept hidden in my room
One year's labors worth
Of the finest of perfumes.

There is nothing else I have
That is worthy of my Lord
I come where He's reclining
Break the precious box and pour

I worship Him and thank Him
As I anoint His head and feet
Tears fall freely as I praise Him
And the perfume trickles onto me

The fragrance of my worship
Saturates the room
My love, my tears, my very heart
Poured out as a perfume

Anysia Derora

I see approval in His eyes
Though my gift seems so very small
I break the box at His feet
to make sure I gave it all

And as I give the very last
And I've done all I could do
I feel His love enfold me
and hear Him say, "I love you, too!"

Matthew 26:7-13

7A woman came up to Him with an alabaster flask of very precious perfume, and she poured it on His head as He reclined at table. 8And when the disciples saw it, they were indignant, saying, "For what purpose is all this waste? 9 For this perfume might have been sold for a large sum and the money given to the poor." 10But Jesus, fully aware of this, said to them, "Why do you bother the woman? She has done a noble (praiseworthy and beautiful) thing to Me. 11 For you always have the poor among you, but you will not always have Me. 12 In pouring this perfume on My body she has done something to prepare Me for My burial. 13 Truly I tell you, wherever this good news (the Gospel) is preached in the whole world, what this woman has done will be told also, in memory of her."

My Promised Land

You are my glory
And the lifter of my head
You write my story
Direct my journey
And You are my Promised Land

You're my exceeding great reward
You are my shield and my strength
You surround me with singing and with joy
You permeate my life with peace
Your perfect love casts out all fear
And You are my Promised Land
You are my Promised Land

Your river of delights flows to me freely
And I hear Your invitation
"Child, come drink deeply."
As Your favor surrounds me and my cup overflows
I'm overcome
By Your peace and love
That I've finally come to know
Jesus
You are my Promised Land
Jesus, You are my Promised Land

Key: You were Made to...

Beloved, you are created in My image!

You were made to be radiant, shining brightly with My love and My glory!

You were made to walk in newness of life every day!

To explore My height, depth, breadth and length and to invite others to join you on the journey.

Every day is supposed to be an exhilarating journey; unparalleled to anything ever experienced before.

Every day is supposed to be a new adventure in Me; full of new revelation; fresh insight; greater wisdom and depth of understanding; nearer to My heart; fulfilling My desire in it.

You were made to lack for nothing.

You were made to walk above circumstances, situations and so-called problems.

You were made to be continually victorious in all things.

You were made to triumph.

You were made to occupy and take more and more ground.

You were made to overcome!

You were made to walk in freedom and liberty!

You were made to sing, rejoice, dance, give thanks and delight every single day of your life. You were made to enjoy My presence. To walk with Me and know Me personally and intimately.

You were made to live in power, authority and dominion.

You were made to love - lavishly and liberally and without fear! And you were made to receive love just as lavishly, just as liberally and just as fearlessly.

You were made to be adored and delighted in.

You were made to participate, engage and enjoy life in all its fullness. Not as the world defines life but as I do!

You were made to be adored and delighted in!

Remember Who You Are

Remember who you are
A child of the King
Remember who you are
Destined to do great things
Remember who you are
Purchased with a price
Remember who you are
Brought from darkness into light
Remember who you are
Known by name from birth
Remember who you are
Conqueror of earth
Remember who you are
Boldly standing before God
Remember who you are
And again, who you are not

You are the spotless bride of Christ
To this world, you are His light
His letter to all with ears to hear
Called to freedom, never fear
You are the child of the King
You are His hands, you are His feet
You carry His Spirit of grace and power
Born to live this very hour
You were hand chosen for today
To show the world the Living Way
To touch the ones no one else sees
To love them to eternity
You are the carrier of the Words of Life
Full of grace and strength and might

They won't hear if you don't go
You'll never leave if you don't know
You are His way to reach their heart
You are His greatest work of art
Not one day are you alone
You are the seed that God has sown

To live life consecrated, set apart
You must remember who you are

I Am Your Promised Land

I am
Your Promised Land
I am your reward
I am
your Prince of Peace
your Counselor in War

I walk beside you
I am with you
You are not alone
You're in Me
And I'm in you
Forever

I am your Promised Land
I am your place of rest
I am Your purity
and your righteousness
I am, I am
I am your Promised Land

I am your portion
your glory,
the lifter of your head
your inheritance
your life, your joy
I am your Promised Land
I am, I am
I am your Promised Land

I walk beside you
I am with you
You are not alone
You're in Me
And I'm in you
Forever

You are flesh of My flesh
You are bone of My bone
You're My delight
And My desire is for you
Here I am
Here I am
I am your Promised Land
Beloved here I am
I am
Your Promised Land

"I Am Your Promised Land" is a song I heard the Lord singing over me at the "Making a Prophetic Impact" conference which Graham Cooke held in Portland in May of 2015. It was a life-changing conference for me and this revelation thrilled and delighted my heart.

Have you ever thought about it? Your promised land is God Himself! That means He is the Provider as well as the Provision. He is your abundance. He is your sustenance. He is your dwelling place. In Him you truly live and breathe and have your being. Everything in your life is in Him if you have accepted Jesus as your Lord and Savior.

The thought still has me in awe! The song "My Promised Land" was my response to Him singing this song over me. There have been many times that He has sung this to me since then, and I delight in His delight to remind me continually just how enmeshed my life is in His.

Key: Burn

It is time for you to allow the fire I have placed in you to be poured out.

Don't be afraid to burn! You will not be consumed, but you will be transformed in its blaze.

Arise in your authority, power and gifting and refuse to give place to fear.

Step out of the boat in faith and I will surely meet you.

I have already made full provision for every step along the way.

Come, be poured out and burn brightly as you were meant to.

I Am With You

Do not be troubled
or frightened
be not worried
or dismayed
I am right here
with you
do not be afraid.
I will lead you.
I will guide you.
I will make
your way clear.
Go forth in strength.
Go forth in power.
Go forth in love
and do not fear.
I have made
your way straight.
I have made
your feet sure.
You will not be shaken
In Me,
you stand secure.
Do not be troubled
or be frightened
be not worried
or dismayed
I am always with you.
do not be afraid.

One thing I've learned about God over the years is that He has no problem coming to us in our times of trial or transition and reminding us of His promise and His presence.

It is an unspeakable comfort to me to hear Him remind me, as He did in **"I Am with You"** that He is with me, He will lead me and guide me and He always, always makes a way.

I'm so grateful for His patient love and continual presence – regardless of how situations look or how I feel.

Psalm 5:11

But let all those who take refuge *and* put their trust in You rejoice; let them ever sing *and* shout for joy, because You make a covering over them *and* defend them; let those also who love Your name be joyful in You *and* be in high spirits.

Relentless God

Rock of my refuge
High tower, my defense
Exceeding great reward
My shield and song

Impenetrable fortress
Delighted lover of my soul
Relentless God
Who's singing over me

When I cried, "My foot is slipping,"
You rushed in with loving-kindness
Your tender mercies
Drew me to Your arms

You have been my help, oh Lord
You have held me up
I dwell beneath the banner
Of Your fierce and ceaseless love

Rock of my refuge
High tower, my defense
Exceeding great reward
My shield and song

Impenetrable fortress
Delighted lover of my soul
Relentless God
Who's singing over me

2nd Corinthians 5:17

Therefore, if any man be in Christ, he is a new creature: old things are passed away; behold, all things are become new.

Nugget: Upgrades

Ephesians 1:19 AMP 19 And [so that you can know and understand] what is the immeasurable and unlimited and surpassing greatness of His power in and for us who believe, as demonstrated in the working of His mighty strength,

God's power in and for us is immeasurable, unlimited and surpassing in greatness and it is DEMONSTRATED in the WORKING of His mighty strength.

The Holy Spirit asked me a question as I pondered this:

"What is going on in your life that feels heavy, overwhelming, too big for you to handle?

What if those things are just opportunities for Me to demonstrate the IMMEASURABLE, UNLIMITED AND SURPASSING GREATNESS of My power in and for you?

How would that thought, that belief, change how you see those things?"

I got a little excited about that because I have some of those things in my life and I realized that He was upgrading how I see circumstances and situations - from things I need to just deal with; to opportunities for Him to show off His great strength and power in my life because He loves me.

What is going on today in your life that feels heavy, overwhelming and too big for you to handle?

What if those things are just opportunities for God to demonstrate the immeasurable, unlimited and surpassing greatness of His power in and for you?

How does that thought impact how you see what's going on in your life?

Higher Than I

When my heart is overwhelmed within me
I cry out to You
You rush in and rescue me
You lift me up

You place my feet upon the Rock
That is higher, so much higher than I am
And You wrap me there in the splendor of
Your sure and perfect love

You lift me high
So I can see the things You see
You draw me near
So I can hear Your song

You raise me up
In Your right hand I dwell safely
You remind me
I've been here all along

On the Rock
That is higher
That is higher
Higher than I

We all go through times where our hearts feel overwhelmed. Regardless of the reason; the feeling is common to us all at some point in time.

I wrote **"Higher than I"** during a time of prayer at church in early 2016. I was praying or trying to but the only words I had were, "Papa, my heart is overwhelmed. Lead me to the Rock that is higher than I."

I really don't know how many times I said it when **"Higher than I"** came pouring out of my mouth. It became my prayer, my praise and my reminder that God has a higher perspective and He is always inviting us up to that place.

No matter how things look or feel; no matter the situation or circumstances, He sees and knows and has promised to work all things together for the good of those who love Him.

Psalm 61:2

From the end of the earth will I cry to You, when my heart is overwhelmed *and* fainting; lead me to the rock that is higher than I [yes, a rock that is too high for me].

Nugget: Breakthrough

*T*his may make you laugh but recently I was talking to the Lord about a breakthrough I needed and was wondering why I didn't have it yet.

He asked me to consider what breakthrough meant to me...and my answer surprised me a little bit - "Breakthrough means that I've walked through the problem and it is now behind and I'm moving forward."

I KNEW that was not the right definition as soon as I said it out loud and I had to grin because I knew the Holy Spirit was about to tell me something really cool and something that I might not really want to hear.

He asked me: *"So, you think that you can continue just walking on your way and experience breakthrough?"*

Without waiting for me to answer He reminded me of a cartoon I saw as a kid where this baby would crawl until it hit a wall and instead of turning around and going another way, the baby would continue trying to crawl, head pressed against the wall, but not moving, until someone picked her up and turned her around. Then she would do the same thing again. I laughed out loud because that's kind of how I felt in this situation.

Then He said this to me: *"Beloved, think about the word 'breakthrough'. Does not even the word itself speak of an intentional violence; demolition; and force? If you want breakthrough in this area, then you need to apply yourself to 'break' through it."*

He let that sink in a few minutes before He continued, *"Don't be surprised if the breakthrough leads you to the front lines of a greater battle, rather than to the place of ease and comfort you're hoping for. In so many cases, the initial breakthrough simply reveals what is really going on, a deeper and more relevant battle. But there's good news! Once you break through initially, you can use that momentum and all you learned to break through that initial battle to secure the territory of your heart and walk in a greater level of victory in the heat of the battle you're thrust into."*

I took it all in, making notes, so that I could continue talking to Him about this when He asked me a final question: *"So, do you want breakthrough in this area enough to do something about it or are you going to keep walking into the wall expecting it to eventually just give way?"*

"I want the breakthrough. I need the breakthrough."

And from that moment, He began unveiling the strategy to do just that.

For weeks I had been walking into the same wall with nothing but a headache to show for it, waiting for God to break the wall down in front of me when all along He was waiting for me to take up the weapons of my warfare; cast down vain imaginations and stop being complacent about what I was dealing with.

Breakthrough requires my participation. Breakthrough is intentional. Breakthrough requires force and a setting of the spirit that will not relent – no matter what's waiting on the other side.

Micah 2:13

The Breaker [the Messiah] will go up before them.
They will break through, pass in through the gate and
go out through it, and their King will pass on before
them, the Lord at their head.

Breaker

I set my eyes on the Breaker
My God, Who breaks through for me
He's gone before me, He is leading me out
In glorious victory

Every wall falls at His appearing
Mountains melt at His voice, rolling thunder
The valleys stand tall to meet Him
Doors of iron and brass cast asunder

Nothing can stand before Him
No one can hinder His plan
Nothing can ever make stumble
The child who He's made to stand

So I set my eyes on the Breaker
On my magnificent King
He's gone before me and opened the way
And my heart gladly follows His lead

He whispers, "You are made in My image,
Allow Me to break forth through you.
Ignite the earth with My glory.
Invite those who hear to The Truth.

Rivers spring forth in the desert.
An oasis in each step you take.
Healing and freedom, love, peace and joy
Banners that are marking the way

Indeed, I have gone before you.
I truly have made all things new.
You are bone of My bone and flesh of My flesh
Allow Me to break forth through you."

So I set my eyes on the Breaker
Wholly set apart for my King
Strengthened with might by His Spirit
Embracing all that He's made me to be.

God's timing never ceases to amaze me! In 2015 I saw someone, who is now a dear friend of mine, using worship flags and her heart and the flags were shifting the atmosphere. I was enthralled. I thought I'd never seen such a beautiful expression of worship or such an intense and glorious change as she just loved on the Lord at the back of the room.

Early in 2016 when I started dancing in worship again, the Lord told me it was time to order the flags. Which I did, with great anticipation! Since the flags are custom made, it can take a while to get them.

The first part of April, God was speaking to me about breakthrough (the Nugget on page 107) and I wrote the poem **"Breaker"**. About 2 weeks later, during my last week at work, my flags arrived and they were named "Breakthrough"! Exactly what I was studying and, not surprisingly, exactly what I needed.

Testimony: Nothing Impossible

"*A*nysia, you have to come to grips with the reality that whatever you were born to be is gone. You will never be whatever that was. … Understand the fact that you will spend the rest of your life on medication and at least half of the rest of your life in a mental hospital. I should put you there now because of those cuts on your arm."

The words cut deeper than whatever I had used to cut my arm with just hours before. Here was a trusted psychiatrist, someone who had worked closely with me to keep me on as many natural sources to manage the various symptoms of Dissociative Identity Disorder (D.I.D.) I was dealing with as possible, now telling me that recovery wasn't possible and that the best I could do was hope for symptom management for the rest of my life. At 34 that was not what I wanted to hear!

A couple days later I was in Juneau, Alaska for a week of revival meetings. I had not intended to go after that psych appointment. Why bother? But I lost all time between the moment I made the decision not to go and the moment I was standing in the airport in Juneau.

To this day I don't recall packing. I only recall the vaguest snippet of the drive to Seattle to fly to Alaska. All I do remember is standing, utterly confused and lost in Juneau telling God, "Obviously You want me around for something but I can't live like this. I will do whatever I have to but I have to be healed."

A lot of that week remains a blur in my mind but what I do remember is this – I took copious notes at the morning and evening revival meetings; noting scriptures; talking to God about them in my heart as I listened; completely open-hearted receiving all that He was saying to me.

Often I went back to the hotel and closed myself in the huge walk-in closet, put my headset on and listened to praise and worship music as I prayed in the Spirit or read the scriptures aloud, holding on to every bit of hope I could get.

Within a couple days I was sleeping through the night and my sleep was sweet and peaceful. Over the next few days, my mind began to heal and God was doing a deep and powerful work in my emotions and soul, while strengthening my spirit. By the end of the week I was healed of the D.I.D.

My healing was certainly supernatural; but there is still a day-to-day walking out of that healing; and other areas of healing that arise in the process as another area is established.

The Lord Himself has continues walking with me through layer upon layer of the restoration and healing process; changing and upgrading my filters from glory to glory; strength to strength. He reveals to me in greater measure what Complete Freedom looks like, acts like, feels like.

Many people have asked me, why God didn't heal everything? If it was God, wouldn't He do it all at once?

I don't have a good answer for that, except to say that His power in healing me of the D.I.D. that serves as a reminder that He is absolutely faithful and intentional to heal me!

Truly, there is no limit to His power and no end to what He will do to show Himself strong on behalf of those who love Him. And absolutely nothing is impossible for our limitless, all powerful God!

Limitless God

Because You are limitless
I am unlimited
according to Your power
working within me
Because You are limitless
I am unlimited
according to Your power
working within me

Taking me higher
Taking me deeper
Drawing me nearer than
I've ever gone before
No looking back to yesterday
Stepping out in this new living way
Holding nothing back
I will press on

Because You are limitless
I am unlimited
according to Your power
working with in me
Because You are limitless
I am unlimited
according to Your power
working within me

Not by might, nor by strength
but by Your Spirit
Not by might, nor by strength
but by Your Spirit
Not by might, nor by strength
but by Your Spirit
Exceedingly abundantly
above all I could ask or think
working mightily in me
You are working
mightily in me

Because You are limitless
I am unlimited
according to Your power
working with in me
Because You are limitless
I am unlimited
according to Your power
working within me

I wrote "Limitless God" at RHEMA's Camp Meeting in 2014. Through each different minister, this theme continued to leap out at me and one day I caught it, and I started singing this song.

I have turned back to this song time and again since I wrote it to remind myself of Who God is for me and what He has given me in Christ through His resurrection.

It is not my own might or strength (thankfully) but His Limitless Spirit that empowers me to live an unlimited life in Him.

Faithful And Intentional To Heal Me

You are faithful and intentional
to heal me
So I come into Your Presence
in this joyful vulnerability
Knowing
You are everything I need

My health, my strength
my joyful song
My wisdom, rest and peace
Victorious Warrior, Conquering One
Glorious, Majestic King of kings
You see me healed
You see me whole and strong
You see me victorious
You see me in Your Son

I stand my ground secure in You
Knowing You have already won
As a well-loved child I rest in You
Recalling Who You are and all You've done

My health, my strength
my joyful song
My wisdom, rest and peace
Victorious Warrior, Conquering One
Glorious, Majestic King of kings
You see me healed
You see me whole and strong
You see me victorious
You see me in Your Son

I say with You - I'm healed
I say with You - I'm whole and strong
I say with You - I'm victorious
Abiding in the fullness of Your Son

Nugget: Fearless Life

*R*ejoicing is a key to a fearless life.

Fear cannot abide long in the heart of one who chooses to worship and magnify God.

It diminishes to nothing as praise and adoration arise to the Lord; and flees in the presence of His glory.

If you want to fear less, rejoice more.

Song of Strong Encouragement

Be strong and courageous
do not fear, know your God
Be strong and courageous
do not fear, know your God

For those who know their God
will do exploits in His name
and they will stand secure
in the day when all things shake

The mountains you are facing now
will bow before My name
I will go in front of you
and make the rough places, straight

Know that I am with you
in everything you do
take this strong encouragement
from heaven

Be strong and courageous
do not fear, know your God
Be strong and courageous
do not fear, know your God

Oh be strong, be strong
be courageous
know your God
do not fear

Daniel 11:32b

...but the people who know their God shall prove themselves strong *ana* shall stand firm and do exploits [for God].

You Are Not Alone

You're not alone when midnight comes
and finds you on your knees again
You're not alone when you're not sure
if you can take another step

You're not alone when the storms rage
and no one is around
You're not alone when the waters rise
and you feel you just might drown
Oh no
Oh no
You are not alone

There are arms longing to embrace you
hands that will not let you fall
There's an ear that hears every word
whispered in your heart
Oh know
Oh know
You are not alone

You're a child of the King of kings,
Ancient of days, the Prince of Peace
A masterpiece formed by the Potters hand
You're a temple of the Living God
Highly favored by the Holy One
Whose made your way and He won't let you go
Oh know
You are not alone
Beloved know
you are not alone

Nugget: Consider it All Joy

James 1:2 AMP Consider it nothing but joy, my brothers and sisters, whenever you fall into various trials.

What trials are you experiencing right now? Can you find something in them that makes you smile or laugh? Can you see what the enemy has meant for evil in them but how God is turning it around for your good?

I encourage you to begin making a list of those things...the good things you are seeing and intentionally rejoice about them. As you do, I believe the Lord will open up your eyes and heart even wider to see more things to smile and laugh about.

In the midst of my own trials I've found myself singing a song I wrote in Bible School in 2006 and revised in 2013. (**"Laugh"** page 69)

May this song serve as a reminder of the beauty and strength of the joy of the Lord and the reality that He is laughing **with** you because He knows the outcome. He has already given you the victory. There is promise and provision all around you and it is His express desire to reveal that to you.

The enemy works with weapons of mass distraction, trying to keep your eyes off of God and what He is doing but know for certain – God will never leave you; He will never forsake you. He will never fail you. And it is His heart's desire to always lead you into victory!

2nd Corinthians 4:17

For our light, momentary affliction (this slight distress of the passing hour) is ever more and more abundantly preparing and producing and achieving for us an everlasting weight of glory [beyond all measure, excessively surpassing all comparisons and all calculations, a vast and transcendent glory and blessedness never to cease!],

Deeper into Praise

In desperation I look to you
I see the end, but no way through
I remind myself of Who You are
And set my gaze upon Your heart

You have gone before me
You have made the way
You've brought the valleys high, the mountains low
Made crooked places straight

I need not fear, for You are with me
I need not fear, You will not leave
I trust in You, Almighty God
Who makes the darkness flee

I behold You in Your glory
In Your wondrous majesty
Here, my heart cries "holy"
And I worship on my knees

There is no other worthy
No god like unto You
There is no other glorious
None faith, kind and true

In the splendor of Your presence
Lost in Your embrace
I realize with wonder
You are my way, my place
And this journey has only ever been
A journey deeper into praise

1st John 4:18

There is no fear in love [dread does not exist], but full-grown (complete, perfect) love turns fear out of doors and expels every trace of terror! For fear brings with it the thought of punishment, and [so] he who is afraid has not reached the full maturity of love [is not yet grown into love's complete perfection].

Strong Habitation

In You, oh Lord, do I place my trust
Let me never be ashamed
Deliver me in Your righteousness
Incline Your ear to my prayer

Be Thou my strong habitation
The place I can run to
Be there, be there for me
Be Thou my strong habitation
Where I can always run
You have given me Your Word
to save me
For You are my rock, my fortress
My deliverer oh God

You are my hope
You are my confidence
You have sustained me from my youth
You are brought me forth
From my mother's womb
So I will give my song to You
And I always praise Your name

Be Thou, oh God, my strong habitation
The place I run and hide
Be Thou, oh God, my strong habitation
You are my rock, my fortress, my God

Psalm 71:1-3 KJV

¹In thee, O LORD, do I put my trust: let me never be put to confusion. ²Deliver me in thy righteousness, and cause me to escape: incline thine ear unto me, and save me. ³Be thou my strong habitation, whereunto I may continually resort: thou hast given commandment to save me; for thou art my rock and my fortress.

The Place of Joy

There's a place in God's presence
Where laughter surrounds you
The glory of God's sheer delight
Where the joy of His heart sings
A boisterous melody
And everything is dancing in light

The tears are all tucked in their bottles
The darkness has long ago fled
You're splashing in rivers of healing
Just the way He said
And you, you are there with Him

You belong in the place
Of joy and singing
Of music and melody
You belong in the place of
outrageous laughter
Wrapped in the joy of Your King

You were made for the glory of heaven
You were made the smile of His heart
There's a place in His presence
Filled up with joy
And that place is where you are
That place is where you are

Nehemiah 8:10 says that the joy of the Lord is our strength and many times I've heard people say that this refers to our laughter and finding joy in Him. But the Lord showed me that that is really only a small part of the meaning of this verse.

Our strength is also found in God's delight in us. His joy in our being His. It is His sheer pleasure and abounding joy in who we are and who we are becoming that is our strength. We are invited to draw our own joy from that boundless well of ceaseless joy unspeakable that the Lord takes in us.

"The Place of Joy" is a song I wrote as a reminder of that amazing truth. God delights in me. God delights in you!

Come and Dine

Come and dine your Father's calling
Come and drink the wine He's pouring
Drink deeply and imbibe of Him
The very best of heaven, is all around
Walking and leaping and praises abound
So come, come and dine
come and drink this new wine
come, oh come
Your Father's calling

The banquet is prepared,
there is joy in the air
as the oil of heaven rains down
every cup is overflowing,
with the new wine He's pouring
so come, oh come your Father's calling

Come and dine, your Father's calling
Come and drink the wine He's pouring
Drink deeply and imbibe of Him
The very best of heaven, is all around
Walking and leaping and praises abound
So come, come and dine
come and drink this new wine
come, oh come
Your Father's calling

Key: Free To

I *want you to understand something: freedom is not only **from** something but it is also **to** something.*

*Yes, I have set you free **from** sin, death, bondage and lies; regret, shame, ashes and heaviness; sickness, disease and poverty but I have also set you free **to** know Me, love Me, and walk in My ways; free **to** lay aside all that is old and walk in complete newness of life.*

*I have set you free **to** come up higher in your thinking, in your living, in your experience of Me in this life.*

*Too many live their lives with their eyes set on the past, on what I have set them free **from** and never see what I have set them free **to**.*

As you shift your focus from the past to the present and future, an amazing and wonderful expanse of the blessing of being Mine will open up before you.

*You are free **to** explore My depths!*

*You are free **to** walk in My power and authority.*

*You are free **to** live in My wisdom and understanding.*

*You are free **to** know the height, depth, length and breadth of My love and to dwell on the earth surrounded by My goodness, favor and blessing.*

*I have set you free **to** live life unlimited in Me.*

*I have set you free **to** experience the fullness of Who I am and **to** live your life from the overflow of that fullness.*

When you stop focusing on what I have set you free from and begin to set your sights on what I have set you free to - everything will change.

You will begin to see differently, speak differently, think differently and live differently. The joy of your salvation will be restored and I will be magnified because you will begin to see Me in a new light, from a new perspective.

You will become rapt with My presence and the precious promises which I have given you by which you are a partaker of My divine nature.

*Beloved, you are free **to** reckon yourself dead to sin but alive unto Me.*

*You are free **to** put off the old man and leave him in the ground and put on Christ, who lives and dwells within you.*

*You are free **to** be who I have called you to be - in all the splendor and wonder that I have woven into you.*

*You are free **to** forget what lies behind and apprehend all that I have apprehended you for.*

*You are free **to** delight in Me and in My presence!*

*You are free **to** partake of life and that more abundant; because you are free **to** partake of Me and I am your life.*

*I invite you, Beloved, to explore the reality of what I have set you free **to** and enjoy the fruit of the discovery that awaits.*

When you stop focusing
on what I have set you free from
and begin to set your sights
on what I have set you free to –
everything will change.

You Speak to Me in Promise

You speak to me in promise
In the certainty of favor
In unfailing strength
In laughter and in love
You speak to me in radiance
In seas of dancing color
On delighted songs and melodies
You lift me up

> The sea is rising
> As deep cries unto deep
> The sea is rising
> As You love me
> How You love me

You speak to me in promise
In majesty and glory
You speak to me in joy
And sheer delight
You speak to me in beauty
In journey and in story
You speak to me
In living words of life

> The sea is rising
> As deep cries unto deep
> The sea is rising
> As You love me
> The sea is rising
> Lifting up my faith
> The sea is rising
> As I love You
> Oh I love You
> Lord I love You
> And I love
> The way
> You speak to me

Psalm 126:1

When the Lord brought back the

captives [who returned] to Zion,

we were like those who dream

[it seemed so unreal].

Anysia Derora

Selah